T0368093

GO, AND TELL IT ON THE MOUNTAIN, DEAR BARBARA, SAYS THE LORD JESUS

BARBARA ANN MARY MACK

authorHOUSE®

AuthorHouse™
1663 Liberty Drive
Bloomington, IN 47403
www.authorhouse.com
Phone: 833-262-8899

Published by AuthorHouse 12/04/2024

ISBN: 979-8-8230-3928-4 (sc)
ISBN: 979-8-8230-3929-1 (hc)
ISBN: 979-8-8230-3930-7 (e)

Library of Congress Control Number: 2024926023

Print information available on the last page.

Any people depicted in stock imagery provided by Getty Images are models, and such images are being used for illustrative purposes only. Certain stock imagery © Getty Images.

This book is printed on acid-free paper.

Because of the dynamic nature of the Internet, any web addresses or links contained in this book may have changed since publication and may no longer be valid. The views expressed in this work are solely those of the author and do not necessarily reflect the views of the publisher, and the publisher hereby disclaims any responsibility for them.

GO, AND TELL IT ON THE MOUNTAIN, DEAR BARBARA, SAYS THE LORD JESUS

BY:

BARBARA ANN MARY MACK

BEGAN: AUGUST 4, 2024
COMPLETED: AUGUST 6, 2024

CONTENTS

ABOUT THE BOOK

GO, AND TELL IT ON THE MOUNTAIN, DEAR BARBARA REVEALS THE AUTHOR'S RELATIONSHIP WITH ALMIGHTY GOD. BARBARA IS COMMISSIONED BY THE CREATOR TO PERFORM A GREAT AND HOLY WORK IN **THE** MIDST OF EARTH'S VALUABLE RESIDENTS. IT IS WRITTEN IN THE FORM OF POETRY, WHICH MAKES IT VERY EASY FOR THE READER TO FOLLOW AND OBTAIN THE MESSAGES THAT ARE CONVEYED.

ABOUT THE AUTHOR

BARBARA ANN MARY MACK IS THE AUTHOR OF OVER 65 GOD INSPIRED PUBLISHED BOOKS, WHICH WERE REVEALED TO HER THROUGH DIVINE DICTATION. BARBARA IS ALSO A TRAVELING MISSIONARY MINISTER AND A DELIVERER OF GOD'S MESSAGES TO SPECIFIC INDIVIDUALS AS THE PROPHETS OF THE PAST. BARBARA'S BOOKS ARE HOLY, AS THE BIBLE IS HOLY. FOR, THE SAME GOD WHO REVEALED HIS WORD TO THE BIBLICAL PROPHETS CONTINUES TO SPEAK TO HIS CHOSEN MESSENGERS TODAY. HE IS OUR ETERNAL FATHER, AND HE WILL ALWAYS REVEAL HIMSELF TO HIS EARTHLY LOVED ONES.

DEDICATION

TO ALMIGHTY GOD, AND LIL B

ACKNOWLEDGMENT

IN THE MIDST OF THE WORLD'S UNITY AND CONFUSION, ALMIGHTY GOD, OUR ORIGIN AND CREATOR, WALKS IN OUR BLESSED MIDST. HE HAS NEVER ABANDONED US, FOR WE ARE HIS GREATEST CREATION. LET US GIVE HIM CONTINUOUS PRAISE-ALLELUIA!!!

BOOK ONE

BOOK ONE

GO, AND TELL IT ON THE MOUNTAIN, DEAR BARBARA, SAYS THE LORD GOD

BY:

BARBARA ANN MARY MACK

INTRODUCTION

<u>THE LORD GOD SPEAKING TO BARBARA</u>

GO! GO! GO, DEAR BARBARA!
SPREAD MY GOOD NEWS TO MY SEARCHING **SON AND DAUGHTER!**

TELL THEM, SO THAT **THEY MAY HEAR-**
THE GOOD NEWS ABOUT THE GOD **WHO IS VERY NEAR.**

GO, DEAR DAUGHTER, **GO TODAY-**
TELL THE WORLD EVERYTHING THAT **ALMIGHTY GOD HAS TO SAY.**

GO AND TELL-
THE HOLY THINGS THAT YOU **KNOW VERY WELL.**

LET MY EARTHLY **LOVED ONES HEAR-**
ABOUT THE HOLY GOD WHO **DOES CARE.**

GO, AND TELL IT, **DEAR BARBARA-**
SHARE THE GOOD NEWS ABOUT **GOD, THE FATHER.**

TELL THEM ABOUT MY **DIVINE CREATION-**
AS I GATHER THE SOULS FROM **EVERY NATION.**

GO, DEAR BARBARA, FOR, IT IS **AN EMERGENCY!**

FOR, THEY NEED TO UNDERSTAND AND BELIEVE IN **CHRIST JESUS' DIVINITY.**

GO, DEAR ONE!
TELL EVERYTHING THAT I REVEAL TO YOU; TO MY LISTENING **DAUGHTER AND SON.**

MAKE HASTE-
DO NOT LET YOUR VALUABLE TIME BECOME AN **UNNECESSARY WASTE!**

GO, GO; GO!
TELL THEM SO THAT **THEY WILL KNOW!**

TELL THEM ABOUT **MY GOOD NEWS-**
AS THEY SIT IN THEIR **CHURCH PEWS.**

FOR, I AM VERY NEAR TO YOU, **DEAR BARBARA-**
AND, I WANT YOU TO SPEAK TO MY **NEEDY SON AND DAUGHTER.**

SPEAK. SPEAK. SPEAK.
REACH MY BLESSED LOVED ONES WHOM MY HOLY SPIRIT DOES SEEK.

FOR, I AM **THE JUST ONE-**
WHO SEEKS THE SOULS OF HIS VULNERABLE **DAUGHTER AND SON.**

HOLY, HOLY, HOLY-
ARE THE CHILDREN OF GOD ALMIGHTY!!!

BARBARA SPEAKING

I WILL SPEAK TO THE HOLY **MOUNTAINS TODAY**-
I WILL SPEAK TO THEM **AS I PRAY**.

FOR, WAY UP ON THE **MOUNTAIN TOP**-
IS A DIVINE LOVE THAT WILL NEVER **LEAVE NOR STOP**.

I WILL SING **SONGS OF PRAISE**-
AS I SALUTE THE CREATOR OF THE HOLY MOUNTAINS
THESE **GLORIOUS DAYS**.

FOR, HOLY, **YOU SEE**-
IS THE CREATOR CALLED **GOD ALMIGHTY**.

REJOICE, O BLESSED MOUNTAIN

BARBARA SPEAKING TO GOD'S BLESSED MOUNTAIN

REJOICE, O **BLESSED MOUNTAIN**-
JOIN THOSE FROM **EVERY NATION!**

FOR, ALMIGHTY **GOD, YOU SEE**-
HAS SENT **OBEDIENT ME**.

AS I CLIMB YOUR MOUNTAIN OF **DIVINE LOVE**-
I WILL REACH OUT TO THOSE WHO SEARCH AND SEEK
SWEET HEAVEN ABOVE.

I WILL SPEAK TO THE HOLY **HILLS TOO**-
FOR, THE WORDS OF GOD HAVE COME **TO RESCUE.**

HE WILL RESCUE **THE FAITHFUL ONES**-
WHO ARE CALLED HIS WORTHY **DAUGHTERS AND SONS.**

HE WILL RESCUE THE WEAK **AND THE SICK**-
FOR, HE HAS A LOVE THAT WILL NEVER **FADE NOR QUIT.**

FOR, **HOLY AND TRUE**-
IS THE GOD WHO CREATED THE MOUNTAINS, ME, **AND
BLESSED YOU.**

HOLY, HOLY, HOLY-
IS THE LOVE OF GOD ALMIGHTY!!!

FOR, HE SEEKS **THE RICH ONES**-
AND HE SEARCHES THE HEARTS OF THE POOR
DAUGHTERS AND SONS.

HE IS **MEEK**-
AND HE WILL SUSTAIN THE HUMBLED ONES **AND THE
WEAK.**

FOR, **HOLY, YOU SEE**-
IS THE LOVE AND PRESENCE OF **GOD ALMIGHTY!!!**

LET THE HOLY MOUNTAINS HEAR ME SPEAK TODAY

Barbara Ann Mary Mack

BARBARA SPEAKING TO GOD'S HOLY MOUNTAINS

LET GOD'S HOLY MOUNTAINS HEAR **ME SPEAK-**
FOR, I HAVE COME WITH A MESSAGE FOR **THE STRONG
AND THE MEEK.**

HEAR, YE; HEAR, YE, HEAR, YE!!!
HEAR THE HOLY WORDS THAT DESCEND FROM **GOD, THE
FATHER, ALMIGHTY!**

FOR, HE **SPEAKS, YOU SEE-**
THROUGH **BLESSED ME.**

LISTEN, O BLESSED **MOUNTAIN-**
LISTEN TO THE HOLY WORDS THAT DESCENDED FROM
SWEET HEAVEN.

FOR, THROUGH **BLESSED ME-**
I WILL SET GOD'S **HOLY WORDS FREE.**

FOR, I WILL **RELEASE-**
THE HEAVEN SENT WORDS ABOUT **DIVINE PEACE.**

FOR, **HOLY, YOU SEE-**
IS THE REALM OF PEACE THAT COMES FROM **LIFE
GIVING GOD ALMIGHTY.**

REJOICE, O BLESSED MOUNTAIN **OF DIVINE LOVE!**
GIVE PRAISE IN THE PRESENCE OF THE **CREATED STARS
ABOVE.**

OFFER YOUR REALM OF **GRATITUDE**-
AS YOU JOIN THE HEAVEN BOUND **MULTITUDE.**

FOR, **HOLY, YOU SEE**-
IS THE HEAVEN BOUND MULTITUDE THAT SURROUNDS
THE THRONE **OF GOD, THE FATHER, ALMIGHTY.**

HOLY, HOLY, HOLY-
IS THE THRONE OF GOD ALMIGHTY!!!

FOR, HE IS HOLY, AND **HE IS REAL**-
HE IS A LOVE THAT **NO ONE CAN STEAL.**

LET FREEDOM RING IN THE PRESENCE OF GOD'S HOLY
MOUNTAINS TODAY

BARBARA SPEAKING

LET DIVINE **FREEDOM RING**-
IN THE HOLY PRESENCE OF CHRIST JESUS, OUR **DIVINE**
SOVEREIGN KING.

LET FREEDOM RING IN THE PRESENCE OF **GOD'S HOLY**
MOUNTAINS TODAY-
AS I LEAD GOD'S CALLED AND CHOSEN ONES TO HIS
LIFE REWARDING HOLY WAY.

LET THE DIVINE MESSAGES THAT DESCENDED FROM
SWEET HEAVEN-

Barbara Ann Mary Mack

REACH THE LISTENING EARS OF **GOD'S BLESSED CHOSEN.**

FOR, **HOLY, YOU SEE-**
ARE THE MOUNTAINS THAT WERE CREATED BY **GOD, THE ALMIGHTY.**

HOLY, HOLY, HOLY-
ARE THE HEAVENLY MOUNTAINS AND HILLS OF GOD ALMIGHTY.

FOR, THE SEARCHING ONES **DO GATHER-**
IN THE PERFECT PRESENCE OF **GOD, THE FATHER.**

REJOICE, **O BLESSED MOUNTAINS!**
JOIN THE DELIGHTFUL PRAISES OF **GOD'S CHOSEN.**

LORD JESUS: LET YOU AND I SPEAK TO YOUR HOLY MOUNTAIN, SO THAT IT WILL RECEIVE THE PRESENCE OF YOUR WORTHY CHILDREN

BARBARA SPEAKING TO THE LIFE SAVING CHRIST JESUS

LORD JESUS: LET YOU AND I SPEAK TO YOUR MOUNTAIN SO THAT IT WILL RECEIVE THE PRAISES OF **YOUR WORTHY CHILDREN.**

LET THE HOLY MOUNTAIN **REJOICE-**
AS IT HEARS THE PRAISE OF YOUR FAITHFUL CHILDREN'S **UNIFIED VOICE.**

LET US SPEAK, LORD JESUS

BARBARA SPEAKING TO THE LIFE SAVING CHRIST JESUS

LET **US SPEAK**-
TO THE SOULS OF THE ONES **WHOM YOU SEEK**-

FOR, YOUR HOLY WORDS AND **VOICE, LORD JESUS**-
MOVE THE SOULS OF THE OBEDIENT FAITHFUL ONES
AND THE RIGHTEOUS.

HOLY, HOLY, HOLY-
ARE THE SPOKEN WORDS OF CHRIST JESUS, THE
ALMIGHTY!!!

HOLY IS THE **MOUNTAIN**-
THAT UNITES ITS PRAISE WITH **GOD'S CHOSEN.**

FOR GOD'S CHOSEN **ONES, YOU SEE**-
WILL JOIN THE HEAVENLY **MULTITUDE AND ME.**

HOLY, HOLY, HOLY-
ARE THE SPOKEN WORDS OF CHRIST ALMIGHTY!!!

I CAN HEAR THEIR **SWEET MELODY**-
I CAN HEAR THEM AS THEY JOIN THEIR ORIGIN AND
CREATOR; **GOD, THE ALMIGHTY.**

I CAN HEAR YOUR LOVELY MOUNTAINS AS THEY SING
THEIR **SONGS OF PRAISE.**

Barbara Ann Mary Mack

I CAN HEAR THEIR SOUNDS DURING THESE BLESSED GOD SEEKING DAYS.

FOR, HOLY AND TRUE-
ARE THE SONGS OF PRAISE TO YOU.

HOLY, HOLY, HOLY-
ARE THE PRAISES TO GOD ALMIGHTY!!!

YOUR HOLY MOUNTAINS ARE CALLING ME, O GREAT AND HOLY ONE

BARBARA SPEAKING TO ALMIGHTY GOD, THE FATHER

YOUR HOLY MOUNTAINS ARE CALLING ME, O GREAT AND HOLY ONE.
I CAN HEAR THE SOUND OF CHRIST JESUS, YOUR ONLY BEGOTTEN SON.

I CAN ALSO SEE HIM, AS HE BECKONS TO ME.
I CAN REALLY SEE THE FOREVER-LIVING CHRIST JESUS, THE ALMIGHTY.

I CAN HEAR THE SOUNDS OF GOD'S HOLY MOUNTAINS AS THEY CALL OUT TO ME.
I CAN HEAR THE SOUND OF ALMIGHTY GOD, THE BLESSED TRINITY.

WILL THEY LISTEN, O LORD? WILL THE HILLS AND THE MOUNTAINS LISTEN TO US?

<u>BARBARA SPEAKING TO THE LORD GOD</u>

WE HAVE **SPOKEN-**
TO THE HOLY HILLS AND **MOUNTAIN.**

WILL IT BE **HEARD-**
THE RELEASE OF YOUR **HOLY WORD?**

WILL THE BOWING **MOUNTAIN-**
JOIN YOUR PRAISING **CHILDREN?**

WILL THEY **SPEAK-**
TO THE SOULS THAT YOU AND I **SEEK?**

FOR, **HOLY AND TRUE-**
ARE THE WORDS THAT ARE **SPOKEN BY YOU.**

WHEN THE HILLS AND THE HOLY MOUNTAINS BOW

<u>BARBARA SPEAKING TO THE LORD GOD</u>

OH HOLY **GOD ABOVE-**
I CAN SEE THE HILLS AND THE HOLY MOUNTAINS AS
THEY BOW IN THE MIDST OF YOUR SWEET **DIVINITY AND
LOVE.**

<u>BARBARA SPEAKING</u>

I CAN **SEE IT ALL-**
I CAN EVEN SEE THE SOULS WHO ARE ABOUT TO
EXPERIENCE A GREAT **UNHOLY FALL.**

I CAN SEE-
THOSE WHO TRULY SERVE **CHRIST ALMIGHTY.**

I CAN SEE-
GOD'S DIVINE **CREATED BEAUTY-**

I CAN SEE **THE JOY-**
THAT SURROUNDS THE BLESSED LITTLE **GIRL AND BOY.**

I CAN SEE-
THE SPIRITUAL AND VISIBLE PRESENCE OF **GOD ALMIGHTY.**

FOR, ALMIGHTY **GOD, YOU SEE-**
GRANTED THIS MIRACULOUS OCCURRENCE AND **EXPERIENCE TO ME.**

FOR, **HOLY, YOU SEE-**
IS THE CHOSEN MESSENGER (BARBARA) OF **GOD ALMIGHTY.**

HOLY AND REAL-
ARE THE VISIBLE EXPERIENCES THAT I DID **SEE AND FEEL.**

BARBARA SPEAKING TO THE DESCENDED MOUNTAIN

MOVE WITH ME, O BLESSED DESCENDED MOUNTAIN OF **DIVINE LOVE.**

MOVE WITH ME, AS I DANCE AND GIVE PRAISE TO THE ONE WHO **MOVES IN SWEET HEAVEN ABOVE.**

FOR, HIS HOLY **MOVEMENTS, YOU SEE-**
BRING JOY TO MY MIND, SOUL, AND **BLESSED BODY.**

MOVE WITH ME, AS I ENTER THE REALM OF **SWEET DIVINITY.**
MOVE WITH ME, AS I GIVE PRAISE AND HOMAGE TO OUR GREAT AND **HOLY GOD ALMIGHTY.**

MOVE, O BLESSED **MOUNTAIN-**
MOVE IN THE PRESENCE OF ALMIGHTY GOD'S **GREATEST CREATION.**

GIVE CONTINUOUS PRAISE, O BLESSED HILLS. BOW IN THE PRESENCE OF **DIVINE ROYALTY-**
AS YOU MOVE WITH ME IN THE PRESENCE OF ALMIGHTY GOD; **SWEET INFINITY.**

MOVE, O ROYAL MOUNTAIN OF **DIVINE LOVE.**
GIVE PRAISE TO THE HOLY ONE WHO DESCENDED FROM **HIS MIGHTY THRONE ABOVE.**

MOVE, MOVE, MOVE THROUGHOUT **THE NIGHT-**
AS YOU KEEP SWEET HEAVEN WITHIN **YOUR BLESSED SIGHT.**

MOVE THROUGHOUT **THE DAY**-
AS YOU FOLLOW ME TO CHRIST JESUS' LIFE REWARDING
HOLY WAY.

MOVE, O BLESSED **MOUNTAIN:** MOVE WITH DIVINE
GLADNESS!
MOVE, O BLESSED HILLS, FOR YOU ARE IN THE PRESENCE
OF HOLINESS.

MOVE, O BLESSED HILLS. **MOVE TODAY**-
MOVE O PRAISING ONE, AND FOLLOW CHRIST JESUS'
LIFE-SAVING WAY.

AND WHEN CHRIST THE ROYAL KING BECKONS ME

BARBARA SPEAKING

WHEN CHRIST, THE TRUE LIVING KING, **BECKONS ME**-
I WILL GO TO THE MOUNTAIN TOP AND **PROCLAIM HIS
VICTORY.**

HIS **VICTORY**-
SETS HIS EARTHLY **LOVED ONES FREE.**

HIS VICTORY; HIS **TRIUMPHANT VICTORY**-
GLORIFIES THE BELIEVING **ONES AND ME.**

FOR, **HOLY AND REAL**-
IS THE VICTORY OF CHRIST JESUS, THE ALMIGHTY, **THAT
WE CAN FEEL.**

HOLY, HOLY, HOLY-
IS THE VICTORY OF THE FOREVER-LIVING CHRIST
ALMIGHTY!!!

HOLY, HOLY, HOLY-
IS THE REALM THAT RELEASED THE HOLY MOUNTAINS
AND HILLS OF GOD, THE ALMIGHTY!!!

AND, I COMMANDED THE HOLY MOUNTAINS AND HILLS
TO MOVE, SAYS THE LORD JESUS

THE LORD JESUS SPEAKING

MOVE, MOVE, **MOVE WITH ME**-
MOVE, O BLESSED MOUNTAINS, FOR YOU ARE IN THE
HOLY PRESENCE OF **DIVINE HEAVEN SENT ROYALTY.**

MOVE WITH **DIVINE GRACE**-
AS YOU BEHOLD THE BEAUTY OF MY **GLORIOUS AND
RADIANT FACE.**

MOVE, O WONDERFULLY MADE **HOLY HILL.**
MOVE IN THE HOLY PRESENCE OF HE WHOM YOU HONOR
HIS HOLY WILL.

MOVE WITH **DIVINE GRACE**-
AS YOU SURRENDER TO THE PRESENCE AND DOMINANCE
OF THIS **NEEDY HUMAN RACE.**

Barbara Ann Mary Mack

MOVE, O BLESSED **DIVINE CREATION**-
COME AND JOIN THE GOD WHO RULES AND REIGNS OVER
EVERY **BLESSED NATION.**

FOR, **HOLY, YOU SEE**-
IS MY REALM OF **DIVINE ROYALTY**-

MOVE, MOVE, **MOVE, O GREAT CREATION OF MINE!**
MOVE IN MY HOLY PRESENCE DURING THIS **WONDERFUL
PERIOD OF TIME.**

FOR, THE BELIEVING **ONES, YOU SEE**-
HAVE JOINED THE HOLY **ETERNAL GOD ALMIGHTY.**

HOLY, HOLY, HOLY-
IS THE LIVING PRESENCE OF GOD ALMIGHTY!!!

FOR, **I AM REAL!**
I AM THE HOLY PRESENCE THAT NO ONE CAN **IMITATE
NOR STEAL.**

WITNESS ME-
WITNESS AND BEHOLD **MY DIVINITY.**

FOR, **I DO EXIST.**
I, THE LORD JESUS, AM IN YOUR VALUABLE BLESSED
MIDST; I AM IN **EARTH'S SPIRITUALLY NEEDY MIDST.**

AND GOD'S BLESSED MOUNTAINS RECEIVED ME.

THEY, GOD'S HOLY MOUNTAINS, BOWED IN THE PRESENCE OF **THE SENT MESSENGER (BARBARA) OF GOD ALMIGHTY-**
AS GOD'S BLESSED MOUNTAINS **RECEIVED ME.**

I JOINED GOD'S HOLY MOUNTAINS AS WE BECAME UNIFIED AS **ONE BLESSED ENTITY-**
AS WE BOWED IN THE MIDST AND HOLY PRESENCE OF **GOD'S SWEET DIVINITY.**

BARBARA SPEAKING TO GOD'S HOLY MOUNTAINS

BOW IN THE MIDST AND HOLY PRESENCE OF **GOD'S DIVINITY-**
FOR, YOU HAVE BEEN FORMED BY THE GRACE AND POWER OF **THE ALMIGHTY.**

BOW WITH ME, O PRECIOUS HOLY MOUNTAINS, WHO WERE **CREATED FROM DIVINE LOVE.**
BOW WITH ME, O BLESSED MOUNTAIN, FOR WE ARE IN THE HOLY PRESENCE OF HE WHO HAS DESCENDED TO US FROM **SWEET HEAVEN ABOVE.**

FOR, **HOLY AND TRUE-**
IS THE GOD WHO FORMED **BLESSED YOU.**

HOLY, HOLY, HOLY-
IS OUR GREAT CREATOR; GOD ALMIGHTY!!!

UNITE WITH ME-
FUSE WITH THE DAUGHTER AND MESSENGER OF **GOD
ALMIGHTY.**

FOR, HE IS THE **ALMIGHTY HOLY ONE.**
HE IS JEHOVAH GOD'S LIFE **REWARDING VICTORIOUS SON.**

HOLY, HOLY, HOLY-
**ARE THE MESSENGER AND MOUNTAINS THAT BOW IN THE
HOLY PRESENCE OF SWEET INFINITY; GOD ALMIGHTY!!!**

TELL IT. TELL IT. TELL IT.

BARBARA SPEAKING

TELL IT! TELL IT! TELL IT-
TELL IT TO THE CHILDREN WHO FOLLOW **GOD'S HOLY
SPIRIT.**

TELL IT, O GREAT **HOLY MOUNTAIN!**
TELL IT, SO THAT THE WORLD WILL WORSHIP GOD AS
ONE **UNIFIED HOLY NATION.**

TELL OF **HIS GOODNESS-**
TELL OF **HIS HOLINESS-**

TELL OF HIS **JUSTICE AND FAME.**
SPEAK, SPEAK, SPEAK, O BLESSED MOUNTAINS; **SPEAK
OF HIS GLORIOUS NAME.**

TELL IT, O BLESSED MOUNTAIN **OF DIVINE JOY!**
TELL IT TO EVERY BELIEVING **LITTLE GIRL AND BOY.**

FOR, **HOLY AND TRUE-**
IS THE GOD WHO **CALLED YOU.**

SPEAK, SPEAK, **SPEAK LOUD AND CLEAR.**
SPEAK VERY LOUD, DEAR, MOUNTAIN, SO THAT ALL
MAY **LISTEN AND HEAR.**

I WILL JOIN YOUR **WORDS OF PRAISE-**
AS YOU SPEAK THROUGHOUT THESE **GLORIOUS DAYS.**

FOR, **HOLY AND TRUE-**
IS THE GOD WHO HAS BLESSED **ME AND YOU.**

PROCLAIM **THE REALITY-**
OF THE EXISTING **GOD ALMIGHTY.**

PROCLAIM. PROCLAIM. **PROCLAIM.**
PROCLAIM HIS HOLY **UNENDING NAME.**

FOR, **HOLY, YOU SEE-**
ARE OUR PRAISES TO THE LIVING **GOD ALMIGHTY.**

GO, AND TELL IT ON MY HOLY MOUNTAIN, DEAR BARBARA

THE LORD GOD SPEAKING

GO, AND TELL IT ON MY HOLY MOUNTAIN, **DEAR BARBARA.**

Barbara Ann Mary Mack

REVEAL THE HOLY INFINITE GOOD NEWS THAT COME FROM **ME, YOUR CREATOR.**

TELL THE **WHOLE WORLD-**
TELL EVERY SPIRITUALLY LIVING EXCITED **BOY AND GIRL.**

SHARE OUR UNENDING **LOVE STORY-**
THAT COMES WITH KNOWING ME, THE KING OF **HEAVENLY GLORY.**

TELL THE MOUNTAINS, AND REPORT TO MY HOLY HILLS.
TELL ALL OF MY BLESSED **LOVED ONES-**
TELL MY WORTHY **DAUGHTERS AND SONS.**

TELL THEM, **DEAR BARBARA-**
TELL THEM OF THE REALITY THAT YOU SHARE WITH ALMIGHTY GOD, **YOUR LIVING SAVIOR.**

TELL THEM ABOUT **YOUR DIVINE CREATOR-**
TELL THEM ABOUT ME, YOUR INFINITE **GOD AND SAVIOR.**

TELL THEM OF **THE REALITY-**
TELL THEM ABOUT THE LOVE THAT YOU SHARE WITH CHRIST **JESUS, THE ALMIGHTY.**

TELL THE **MOUNTAIN-**
TELL THEM: TELL **MY HOLY LAND-**

FOR, I AM REAL, **DEAR CHILDREN.**

Go, and tell it on the Mountain, Dear Barbara, Says The Lord Jesus 21

MY REALITY WALKS IN THE MIDST OF **MY GREATEST CREATION.**

TELL THE **MOUNTAINS-**
SPEAK OF MY HOLY EXISTENCE TO **THE BLESSED NATIONS.**

LIFT UP **YOUR VOICES-**
AS YOUR UNIFIED EXISTENCE **REJOICES.**

TELL THE MOUNTAINS, **DEAR BARBARA-**
REJOICE WITH THE HOLY LANDS, **DEAR DAUGHTER.**

BARBARA SPEAKING TO GOD'S HOLY MOUNTAINS

OH, THE HOLY MOUNTAINS THAT **DESCENDED IN MY MIDST-**
GIVE CREDENCE TO THE MIGHTY POWER OF OUR LORD GOD WHO NOW MOVES IN OUR BLESSED MIDST; FOR **HE TRULY DOES EXIST.**

FOR, GOD'S HOLY POWER AND PRESENCE **MOVES, YOU SEE-**
IN THE MIDST OF **YOU AND ME.**

MOVE, O BLESSED MOUNTAINS OF **DIVINE LOVE-**
MOVE IN THE HOLY POWER AND PRESENCE THAT DESCENDED FROM **SWEET HEAVEN ABOVE.**

Barbara Ann Mary Mack

FOR, **HOLY AND REAL-**
IS THE UNENDING POWER THAT THE BELIEVING ONES
CAN **TRULY SEE AND FEEL.**

HOLY, HOLY, HOLY-
ARE THE MANY POWERS OF GOD ALMIGHTY!!!

O BLESSED MOUNTAINS THAT WERE CALLED INTO **HOLY**
EXISTENCE-
COME WITH ME, AS I UNITE WITH YOU IN **GOD'S HOLY**
PRESENCE.

FOR, HIS HOLY PRESENCE IS **VAST AND STRONG-**
FOR, HE GIVES SUPPORT AND COMFORT TO THE LIVING
ALL DAY LONG.

HOLY, HOLY, HOLY-
IS THE FOREVER-LIVING CHRIST ALMIGHTY!!!

BOOK TWO

O HOLY NIGHT

O HOLY NIGHT

BY:

BARBARA ANN MARY MACK

BEGAN: NOVEMBER 22, 2024
COMPLETED: NOVEMBER 22, 2024

O HOLY NIGHT

OH WHAT A WONDERFUL AND PEACEFUL NIGHT

INTO THE PEACEFUL AND **SERENE NIGHT-**
I CLING TO THE HOLY BABE WITHIN **MY GLORIOUS SIGHT.**

FOR, HE IS OUR HEAVEN **DESCENDED KING-**
WHO HAS COME BACK TO EARTH AT THIS TIME, SO
THAT HE MAY INTRODUCE EARTH'S RESIDENTS TO **THE
FATHER'S GLORIOUS THING.**

FOR, **HOLY, YOU SEE-**
IS THE BABE WHO HAS COME TO DWELL IN THE BLESSED
MIDST OF **EARTH'S RESIDENTS AND ME.**

FOR, **CHRIST JESUS-**
IS THE HOLY BABE WHO HAS **COME BACK TO US.**

ON THIS **HOLY NIGHT-**
BABY JESUS APPEARED TO ME IN THE FORM OF **A
GLORIOUS LIGHT.**

OH, **HOW EXCITING-**
TO BE IN THE GLORIOUS PRECIOUS OF OUR ROYAL BABY
JESUS; **HEAVEN'S SENT SAVIOR AND KING.**

FOR, **HOLY AND TRUE-**

IS THE KING WHO DESCENDED FROM SWEET HEAVEN TO ME AND **BLESSED YOU.**

HOLY, HOLY, HOLY-

IS THE DESCENDED ROYAL KING AND BABY; CHRIST JESUS, THE ALMIGHTY!!!

O HOLY NIGHT-

PLEASE KEEP THE LORD JESUS WITHIN **MY NEEDY SIGHT.**

FOR, I **DESIRE TO SEE-**

THE GOD AND KING WHO HAS COME BACK TO OFFER SALVATION TO **HIS EARTHLY LOVE ONES AND BLESSED ME.**

FOR, **SALVATION-**

CAN ONLY BE OBTAINED THROUGH THE GOD AND ORIGIN OF **DIVINE CREATION.**

HOLY, HOLY, HOLY-

IS OUR SAVING GOD ALMIGHTY!!!

LORD JESUS-

ON THIS HOLY NIGHT, I WILL CLING TO THE HOLY PRESENCE OF THE **GOD WHO HAS RETURNED TO BLESSED US.**

FOR, **HOLY AND TRUE-**
IS THE BABE WHO HAS COME BACK TO **ME AND YOU.**

ALTHOUGH CHRIST, THE KING, HAS COME TO EARTH IN
THE FORM OF **A NEW BABE-**
HE STILL HAS THE POWER TO GOVERN US **AND SAVE.**

FOR, **HOLY, YOU SEE-**
IS THE HEAVEN DESCENDED GOD IN THE FORM OF **A
HUMAN BABY.**

HE IS ALMIGHTY **GOD, CHRIST JESUS-**
HE IS THE ROYAL KING WHO HAS COME **TO SAVE US.**

HE IS HOLY-
FOR, HE CAME FROM THE HOLY ETERNAL ESSENCE OF
GOD, THE FATHER, ALMIGHTY.

HE IS THE MIGHTY **ROYAL ONE-**
FOR, HE IS GOD, THE FATHER'S, **ONLY BEGOTTEN SON.**

O HOLY NIGHT-
PLEASE KEEP OUR BLESSED SAVIOR WITHIN **MY NEEDY
SIGHT.**

FOR, I LONG **TO EMBRACE-**
THE GLORY THAT SHINES ON **HIS HOLY FACE.**

O HOLY KING-
I BLESS YOU FOR COMING TO EARTH, AND FOR **SHARING.**

FOR YOU **DO SHARE**-
THE GOODNESS OF THE HEAVENLY FATHER AND HIS
HOLY ANGELS WHO **DO CARE.**

MY SOUL IS **TRULY**-
GRATEFUL TO **GOD ALMIGHTY.**

FOR HE HAS SENT HIS **ONLY BEGOTTEN SON**-
TO SHARE A DIVINE LOVE THAT **HAS JUST BEGUN.**

HOLY, HOLY, HOLY-
IS THE GIFT OF LOVE THAT DESCENDED WITH BABY
JESUS, WHICH CAME FROM GOD, THE FATHER,
ALMIGHTY!!!

DURING THE **HOLY NIGHT**-
THE LORD JESUS SHINES THROUGH MY HOME LIKE A
BRILLIANT LUMINOUS LIGHT.

HOLY, HOLY, HOLY-
IS THE BRILLIANCE OF THE LORD JESUS' HEAVENLY
GLORY.

FOR, **HOLY, YOU SEE**-
IS THE BRILLIANCE THAT SURROUNDS CHRIST JESUS,
THE **HEAVEN SENT ALMIGHTY.**

FOR, HE IS TRULY THE GREAT **KING OF KINGS**-
AND HIS HOLY SPIRIT AND PRESENCE SHOWER US WITH
WONDERFUL THINGS.

HE IS THE **DIVINE LIGHT-**
THAT PIERCES EARTH'S **DARKEST NIGHT.**

HOLY, HOLY, HOLY-
IS THE GLORIOUS NIGHT THAT REVEALED THE NEEDY
PRESENCE OF CHRIST JESUS, THE FOREVER-LIVING GOD
ALMIGHTY!!!

LORD JESUS-
I BLESS YOU FOR LEAVING THE COMFORT OF YOUR
HEAVENLY HOME, SO THAT YOU MAY **AGAIN, LIVE**
AMONG US.

IN YOUR **HOLY PRESENCE-**
I LOOK FORWARD TO DWELLING IN YOUR **HEAVENLY**
RESIDENCE.

FOR YOU, O HOLY **KING OF KINGS-**
HAVE COME TO REVEAL GOOD **HEAVEN SENT TIDINGS.**

I WILL CLING-
TO YOUR WONDERFUL **GLORIOUS THING.**

FOR **HOLY AND TRULY-**
IS MY LOVE FOR THE DESCENDED **CHRIST ALMIGHTY.**

FOR, THROUGH THE DARKEST **HOLY NIGHT-**
CHRIST JESUS PIERCED EARTH'S VISIBLE REALM WITH
HIS GLORIOUS BEAMING POWERFUL LIGHT.

HOLY, HOLY, HOLY-
IS THE GLORY OF GOD ALMIGHTY.

FOR HE OFFERS, YOU SEE-
HIS SALVATION TO YOU AND ME.

FOR, HOLY AND TRUE-
IS THE BABY GOD WHO WAS SENT FROM SWEET HEAVEN
TO ME AND YOU.

HOLY, HOLY, HOLY-
IS THE VISIBILITY OF CHRIST ALMIGHTY!!!

FOR, HE MOVES, YOU SEE-
IN THE BLESSED MIDST OF MY BLESSED FAMILY AND ME.

AS I LIE AWAKE IN MY BED AT NIGHT-
I PONDER OVER KING JESUS' GLORIOUS RETURN AND
HIS MIGHT.

FOR, HIS HOLY SPIRIT DID REVEAL TO ME-
THAT HE HAS RETURNED IN OUR MIDST, SO THAT HE
MAY BE CLOSE TO THE LOVED ONES OF OUR HEAVENLY
GOD AND FATHER ALMIGHTY.

O HOLY NIGHT

PLEASE KEEP BABY JESUS WITHIN MY NEEDY SIGHT!!!

Barbara Ann Mary Mack

FOR, HE IS VERY **PRECIOUS TO ME-**
AND HIS HOLY GOD **AND FATHER ALMIGHTY.**

REACH FOR ME, O BLESSED **SAVING GOD-**
REACH FOR MY NEEDY SOUL AS YOU RESCUE THE
FAITHFUL LOVED ONES OF **GOD ALMIGHTY; MY FIRST
AND LAST LOVE!!!**

HOLY, HOLY, HOLY-
IS THE HEAVEN DESCENDED BABE CALLED CHRIST
ALMIGHTY.

BOOK THREE

O COME ALL YOU FAITHFUL, SAYS THE LORD GOD

BY:

BARBARA ANN MARY MACK

O COME ALL YOU FAITHFUL, SAYS THE LORD GOD

BY:

BARBARA ANN MARY MACK

BEGAN: NOVEMBER 22, 2024
COMPLETED: NOVEMBER 22, 2024

COME. COME. COME, O FAITHFUL ONE

<u>THE LORD JESUS SPEAKING TO EARTH'S RESIDENTS TODAY</u>

COME. COME. **COME, O BLESSED ONE!**
COME, AND ENTER MY HEAVENLY KINGDOM ON EARTH, AS YOU FOLLOW **GOD, THE FATHER'S, FAITHFUL ONLY BEGOTTEN SON.**

DEAR CHILDREN-
FROM EVERY **SANCTIFIED NATION.**

COME TO ME-
SO THAT YOU MAY BEHOLD THE HEAVENLY GIFTS THAT SURROUND THE BEING OF **CHRIST JESUS, THE ALMIGHTY.**

COME TO ME **TODAY-**
COME, O FAITHFUL ONES, AND FOLLOW MY LIFE REWARDING **HOLY WAY.**

I AM **VERY NEAR-**
REMEMBER, O BLESSED ONE; REMEMBER THAT **I AM THE HOLY GOD WHO DOES CARE.**

LOOK UP TO ME-
LOOK UP TO THE HOLY GOD WHO HAS SET YOUR FAITHFUL
TROUBLED SOUL FREE.

COME, DEAR ONE-
ENTER MY REALM THAT IS FILLED WITH HEAVEN
ORCHESTRATED DIVINE FUN.

FOR, I, THE LORD JESUS-
HAVE MANY WONDERFUL HEAVENLY THINGS TO SHARE
WITH MY EARTHLY FAITHFUL ONES AND THE RIGHTEOUS.

COME. COME. COME-
ENTER, O BLESSED ONE, ENTER MY LIFE REWARDING
KINGDOM.

DEAR LITTLE ONE; COME HERE-
FOR, I, THE LORD JESUS, WILL TAKE YOUR OBEDIENT
BLESSED SOUL THERE.

I WILL TAKE YOU TO THE LAND-
THAT IS GOVERNED BY MY LIFE GIVING HAND.

COME AND SEE-
DEAR BLESSED ONE; COME WITH ME.

LISTEN. LISTEN. LISTEN.
LISTEN TO MY HOLY SPIRIT, O BLESSED FAITHFUL
CHILDREN.

FOR, ALMIGHTY GOD, **YOUR HEAVENLY FATHER-**
GETS DIVINE PLEASURE FROM HIS OBEDIENT **AND FAITHFUL SON AND DAUGHTER.**

DEAR CHILDREN: **I AM TRULY GRATEFUL-**
THAT YOU HONOR AND RESPECT YOUR HEAVENLY GOD
WHO IS **TRULY DEVOTED AND WONDERFUL.**

FOR, I HAVE HEARD YOUR MANY PRAYERS **THROUGHOUT THE NIGHT.**
AND, I WANT YOU TO KNOW THAT YOUR FAITHFUL LORD,
GOD, AND KING, HAS ALWAYS KEPT YOU **WITHIN MY HOLY SIGHT.**

I AM YOUR MEEK AND **FAITHFUL GOD-**
WHO SHOWERS HIS CHILDREN WITH **HIS HOLY LOVE.**

COME TO ME IN YOUR **TIMES OF NEED-**
AND I WILL SHOWER YOUR BLESSED SOUL WITH THE
HEAVEN MADE NOURISHMENT THAT **I WILL DISTRIBUTE AND FEED.**

FOR, **HOLY AND TRUE-**
IS THE GOD WHO CREATED **FAITHFUL BLESSED YOU.**

LOOK **UPON ME-**
AND YOU WILL BEHOLD **MY DIVINE BEAUTY.**

LOOK UPON YOUR GLORIOUS **KING OF KINGS-**
FOR, I WILL SHOW YOU MANY **HEAVENLY THINGS.**

FOR, I AM YOUR REFUGE: YOUR **FAITHFUL PLACE**-
LOOK, DEAR CHILDREN: LOOK UPON **MY GLORIOUS FACE.**

FOR, I CAN GIVE YOU ETERNAL **LIFE WITH ME**-
FOR YOU HAVE SERVED THE CHILDREN WHO BELONG TO
THE FATHER ALMIGHTY.

COME TO ME-
COME, O BLESSED ONES, SO THAT YOU MAY **EXPERIENCE
THE HOLY TRINITY.**

FOR, WE **DO EXIST**-
WE, O FAITHFUL ONES, ARE NOW, **IN YOUR MIDST.**

EXPERIENCE **GOD, THE FATHER**-
EXPERIENCE ME, THE FATHER'S ONLY BEGOTTEN SON;
CHRIST JESUS, THE ALMIGHTY.

EXPERIENCE **THE HOLY SPIRIT**-
FOR, HE SPEAKS, SO THAT THE FAITHFUL ONES AND
THE RIGHTEOUS **MAY HEAR IT.**

WE THREE ARE IN AGREEMENT AS **ONE GLORIFIED
ENTITY.**
FOR, WE ARE THE **ETERNAL GOD ALMIGHTY.**

HOLY, HOLY, HOLY-
IS THE BLESSED TRINITY!!!

Barbara Ann Mary Mack

HOLY, HOLY, HOLY-
ARE THE FAITHFUL CHILDREN OF GOD ALMIGHTY!!!

FOR, THE **BLESSED TRINITY-**
TRULY LOVES THE LITTLE ONES WHO ARE FAITHFUL **TO GOD ALMIGHTY.**

HOLY, HOLY, HOLY-
ARE THE FAITHFUL CHILDREN OF GOD ALMIGHTY!!!

LET US SOAR, **O BLESSED ONE-**
FOR, YOU ARE IN THE HOLY PRESENCE OF CHRIST JESUS, **THE FATHER'S, ONLY BEGOTTEN FAITHFUL AND OBEDIENT SON.**

LET US SOAR AS ONE UNIFIED SPIRIT IN THE HOLY PRESENCE OF **OUR GOD AND FATHER-**
SO THAT YOU MAY EXPERIENCE THE JOY THAT COMES WITH KNOWING ME, **YOUR ETERNAL REWARD AND SAVIOR.**

COME, DEAR ONE-
GATHER AROUND MY HOLY SPIRIT, O BELOVED **DAUGHTER AND SON.**

FOR, I, YOUR **LORD AND SAVIOR-**
DESIRE TO SEE MY FAITHFUL LOVED ONES; MY OBEDIENT **SON AND DAUGHTER.**

FOR, HOLY, **ETERNAL AND TRUE-**
IS THE SAVIOR WHO IS **FAITHFUL TOO.**

HOLY, HOLY, HOLY-
IS THE FAITHFUL GOD ALMIGHTY!!!

YOU, O **BLESSED ONES-**
YOU WILL BE PERMITTED TO ENTER THE LAND THAT IS
FLOURISHED WITH THE DIVINITY THAT SURROUNDS MY
OBEDIENT AND FAITHFUL **DAUGHTERS AND SONS.**

FOR, IN MY HOLY **LAND, YOU SEE-**
YOU WILL BE TAUGHT AND GOVERNED BY YOUR FAITHFUL
AND **EVERLASTING KING ALMIGHTY.**

HOLY, HOLY, HOLY-
IS THE LAND THAT IS RULED AND GOVERNED BY THE
ROYAL CHRIST JESUS, THE ALMIGHTY!!!

DEAR CHILDREN-
MY FAITHFUL LITTLE ONES **FROM EVERY NATION.**

WALK WITH ME-
SO THAT YOU MAY EXPERIENCE PURE ETERNAL GLORY
AND MY DIVINITY.

WALK WITH ME-
TO THE LAND THAT IS **ETERNAL AND FREE.**

Barbara Ann Mary Mack

WALK WITH ME THROUGHOUT **EACH BLESSED DAY**-
SO THAT YOU MAY LEARN, OF, AND BEHOLD MY
SANCTIFIED LIFE-SAVING WAY.

WALK WITH ME-
AS I ENTER THE BLESSED HOME OF **GOD, THE FATHER,
ALMIGHTY.**

WALK WITH ME-
SO THAT YOU MAY EXPERIENCE THE DIVINE GRACE
THAT **SURROUNDS THE HOLY TRINITY.**

WALK WITH ME-
SO THAT YOU MAY PERSONALLY **BEHOLD MY DIVINITY.**

FOR, **HOLY AND TRUE-**
IS THE GOD WHO WALKS WITH **FAITHFUL YOU.**

HOLY, HOLY, HOLY-
IS THE FAITHFUL ONE WHO WALKS WITH GOD ALMIGHTY!!!

I WILL TELL MY HOLY FATHER AND GOD ABOUT YOUR
FAITHFULNESS AND DEVOTION-
AS I LEAD HIS **OBEDIENT CHILDREN.**

I WILL TELL HIM **EVERYTHING-**
THAT YOU DO FOR ME; CHRIST JESUS, THE HEAVEN
DESCENDED **DIVINE ROYAL KING.**

FOR, **HOLY AND TRUE**-
IS THE KING WHO HAS **SAVED BLESSED YOU.**

HOLY, HOLY, HOLY-
IS THE SALVATION THAT COMES WITH FAITHFULNESS
TO CHRIST ALMIGHTY!!!

DEAR CHILDREN-
O BLESSED NATION.

KEEP ME WITHIN **YOUR NEEDY SIGHT**-
SO THAT YOU MAY EXPERIENCE A GLIMPSE OF MY
DIVINE **PRESENCE AND MIGHT.**

HOLY, HOLY, HOLY-
IS THE GLORIOUS CHRIST JESUS, THE ALMIGHTY!!!

FOR, YOUR **OBEDIENCE, YOU SEE**-
HAS PLACE YOU ON THE THRONE THAT IS NEXT TO **THE**
LIVING CHRIST ALMIGHTY.

HOLY, HOLY, HOLY-
IS THE LIVING THRONE OF CHRIST ALMIGHTY!!!

ALLELUIA! ALLELUIA! ALLELUIA!!!
ALLELUIA TO ALMIGHTY GOD, THE FATHER, JEHOVAH!!!

Barbara Ann Mary Mack

SOME OF MY OTHER GOD INSPIRED PUBLISHED BOOKS

1. WORDS OF INSPIRATION
2. FATHER, ARE YOU CALLING ME? (CHILDREN'S BOOK)
3. DAUGHTER OF COURAGE
4. A HOUSE DIVIDED CANNOT STAND
5. TASTE AND SEE THE GOODNESS OF THE LORD
6. HUMILITY- THE COST OF DISCIPLESHIP
7. WILL YOU BE MY BRIDE FIRST?
8. ODE TO MY BELOVED
9. FATHER, THEY KNOW NOT WHAT THEY DO
10. IN MY FATHER'S HOUSE (CHILDREN'S BOOK)
11. IN MY GARDEN (CHILDREN'S BOOK)
12. THE BATTLE IS OVER
13. THE GOSPEL ACCORDING TO THE LAMB'S BRIDE
14. THE PRESENT TESTAMENT
15. THE PRESENT TESTAMENT VOL. 2
16. THE PRESENT TESTAMENT VOL. 3
17. THE PRESENT TESTAMENT VOL. 4
18. THE PRESENT TESTAMENT VOL. 5
19. THE PRESENT TESTAMENT VOL. 6
20. THE PRESENT TESTAMENT VOL. 7
21. THE PRESENT TESTAMENT VOL. 8
22. THE PRESENT TESTAMENT VOL. 9
23. THE PRESENT TESTAMENT VOL. 10

Go, and tell it on the Mountain, Dear Barbara, Says The Lord Jesus

Barbara Ann Mary Mack

Go, and tell it on the Mountain, Dear Barbara, Says The Lord Jesus   59

Barbara Ann Mary Mack

Printed in the United States
by Baker & Taylor Publisher Services